Joan

I hope you enjoy the poems

Jesse R. Buckley

Ramblings

by Jesse R. Buckley, III

For . . .

My father Jesse, mother Toni-Ann and my
sister Jennifer, with love

With thanks to:

MaryAnn McCarra – Fitzpatrick for her patience with the editing.

Story Musgrave for inspiring me to think beyond what is seen.

My sister, Jennifer for the inspiration for my poetry.

Thank you for supporting this work!

About the Author . . .

Jesse R. Buckley, III is a self-described imaginative-scientist-author-poet who tested as highly gifted shortly before his fourth birthday. Unsurprisingly, he taught himself to read somewhere around the age of two.

He enjoys building contraptions, creating stories, learning to cook, and engaging in scientific experiments. One day he hopes to be an astronaut, and is still slightly upset that NASA has yet to return his emails.

Creative endeavors will continue.

Baby Penguins

Fluffy white snowballs

In Antarctic light

Locked away in frozen chunks

Between papa's feet

Waiting away for warmth

In frozen wasteland

Playing and tripping

Seeing white ice for miles

This curious, fluffy, tiny, cozy, adorable, warm,
noisy, lovable, amazing, incredible

little baby penguin.

Big to Small

Big,

Over-sized, Tall

Giant, Enormous, Huge,

Big, Medium, Average, Small,

Tiny, Pea-sized, Little,

Undersized, Short,

Small.

Clocks

Clocks tick in the night

So peacefully clicking away

Wind them, set them

Determined

I have a letter for my friend.
From start to end
Just around the road's bend
I am determined.

He moved to Topeka
and I can't get there.
But I can get
to the mailbox
without worry, doubt or fret
I am determined.

They say
"You can't do it!"
"You won't go past the bend!"
But I ignore them
I am determined.

The mailman is determined.
Why can't I be?
There is no reason
I can't do it
I am determined.

So I'm going to the mailbox
skipping 'round the bend.
I put it in and went back home.
How'd I do it?
I was determined.

Summer

High temperatures make

Rain evaporate.

Good picnic weather

My Jacob's Ladder

Watching in amazement
as my ladder clicked
the wood.

Click clack click!
Click clack click!

I see my
little ladder
shove the blocks
down.

Click clack click clack...
Click clack click clack...

My little
ladder pushes
the wood down.

Click,Click,Click,Click.

My ladder
may only be wood
but it's still great...

Click clack click clack click clack click clack.........

It's only wood.......
but my ladder is clicking yet.

Start to End

Start,

Fresh, New,

Exciting, Fun, Jumpy,

Begin, Start, Finish, End,

Tired, Boring, Stopping,

Worn-out, Old,

End.

Spring

Flowers bloom in spring

And seem to smile at the

Sun as it flies away

Music

Music is the message

sent through life

around and around

never dying down

resounding through ocean, mountain and lake

going down into a trench

notes so low

climbing to Everest

just to calm

the world.

The Brutal Battle of Chess

Ah, chess!

Where do I begin?
The brutal battle of Black and White!
A battle that seems to last the night!
Checkmate the king, win the fight!
Move the rook left, not to the right!
Capture the queen, give her a fright!
And take the king away.

Touchdown! The pawn moves one space.
Protection! The king moves!
Offense! The queen strikes!
Defense! The rook moves!
And all for the knight moving in an L!
The king is worried, the queen is gone.
They only have a rook and a pawn.
However, the king is cornered!
The Pawn-to-Queen coronation ends!
The new queen comes in!
The king is in a corner, the queen facing him!
The rook threatens the king if the queen is
captured!

All the rooks and bishops are out of range!
The knights cannot move side-to-side!
The game is won!
Hooray for White!

The Gift of Life

Rubies red and sapphires blue
teal turquoise and white pearl too
gold and silver in mines with heat
shiny quartz from caves deep

Iron ore comes from caves
while gold and silver lies in kings graves
Marble or ivory could be in a game of chess
but chipping all that marble really makes a mess

Tan-gram sets of oak and teak
small rocks at mountain peak

And the life of the night
can give you quite a fright

So search the mountains, search the land
Until you find the gift at hand
Not diamonds, gold, silver or ruby
Not sapphire, quartz, teak or ivory
Not marble, pearl,oak or iron ore
Not even a geode, rock, stone or mountain

Not even the whole world
could equal to
the gift of life.

Winter

Cold snowy weather

Snowflakes fall slowly to the

Quiet little ground

The World

World ,

Ancient, Vast

Moving, Spinning, Changing

Journeys around the Galaxy

Racing, Moving, Traveling

Beautiful, Loving

Home

A Friend

A friend:

is nice to you

does not take advantage of you

is there when you need them

helps each other

helps because they *want* to

looks out for you too

To The President

The
Old

Times
Have
Ended

Peacefully. Our
Reign
Ended
Seven years ago.
In the
Dominican Republic and
Estonia, so
Now we should
Try ruling them once more!

Autumn Leaves

Autumn Leaves, so crisp

floating without a worry

in the Autumnal air

Winter II

Winter

Cold, hard

Biting, roaring, rushing , a

Windy, dark

Season

Moon

Moon

Beautiful, bright

Shinning, sparkling, gleaming

Helps us see

Luna

Whispers

Whispering voices

of the night,

so gentle,

so calm,

so peaceful

Draw

Delightful activity

Rainbows

Art

Wonderful

A Tree

A tree is dark brown.

Trees can have leaves with many colors.

Trees can change colors.

Codes

Codes are fun to make

(Some people just don't know about codes)

Codes are great to make!

Winter Time

A cold time of year

Winter is a time of snow and

Skating on the pond

Planets

Uranus, tilted

Jupiter, King of planets

Pluto, the smallest

The End of the World

The ground is leaving

the world, while it will destroy

itself with magma

Our Only Hope

The world is disappearing
the ground lifts away
there is no more weather
it's the end of all the days

The tornadoes whizzing
the air leaving
the tsunamis flowing
the world will have
meaning no more

Wait! There is hope

we all must plant a tree
that's the least we can
do to live on our planet
of blue and green

Unrealized Work

As time goes on
it seems to slow
without songs, poems
and stories being born

Almost as if
there are no more
stories to tell,
poems to recite,
songs to sing

Songs left missing
lyrics, chords, notes
end abruptly
Poems are left
unfinished
untitled
Stories
undetailed
never finished.

Some never written at all

There are so many more stories
to tell
Composers simply don't
realize.

Winter Season

Cold, snowy weather

Snowflakes fall slowly to the

Quiet little ground

Start to End

Start

Fresh, New

Exciting, Fun, Jumpy

Begin, Start, Finish, End

Tired, Boring, Stopping

Worn-out, Old

End.

Computer

Clicking mouse

Over a terabyte in space

Myspace, Facebook, and Twitter

Personal Life

Under $2500

Tricky games and brainteasers

Ending user session

Really cool tech!

Confusing Haiku

Writing a haiku

This is very confusing

Don't know what to do

The Human Brain

The busiest organ
Has a set number of cells
Each is unique

Helps in every way
Undergoes thousands of processes
Make life possible
Almost never fails
No pain sensors

Because of it you can
Read these words
And understand them
In your house
Not with the trilobites!

What is a poem?

A poem is a work of art.

Could it outshine the sun?
Eclipse an eclipse?

Luckier than winning the lottery?
Bigger than space?

More confusing than the 4th dimension?
Darker than nothing?

Harder than diamond?
Sweeter than candy?

To me, a poem is a poem.

But to you, Dear Reader,
that is up to you.

The Tree and the Rescue

Christopher Robin and Elizabeth Ann
wishing they had not ran
sat under a big tree
from which Pooh said others must flee
and there's no up or down
just the way to the tree's crown.

And soon an apple fled
from the top to Elizabeth Ann's head.
"What's this?" Elizabeth Ann said
about the apple that fell on her head.

"Wait! - it's a signal !"

"What's A-sig-enal?" asked Pooh, completely
dazzled.

"A signal, Pooh
is something to
cry for help
without having to yelp.

And we shall go up this tree too." Christopher
Robin said
carrying the apple that hit Elizabeth Ann on the
head.

And so they climbed, and climbed, and climbed,
and climbed

while Christopher Robin recited Twy Stymes.

And they squeezed and squozed and sqoozed
while the sap from the tree oozed.

Finally they reached Piglet who
along with Eeyore was counting sticks too.
"156 . . . 157 . . . 158 . . . 15 . . . OH! Hullo" Piglet
said
as a haycorn hit him on the head.

So they all
(Pooh and Piglet and all)
in the fall
went up the tree
to see
(unexpectedly)
Tigger, Roo, and Rabbit
sitting together as if it were a nasty habit.

When they reached the tree's crown,
they started to climb down.

As they climbed down
everyone started to frown.
They saw the tree
as they could see
it was not the same,

like a modified game.
However, they got through
the entire crew
and got down
from the tree's crown.

Soon they were at the bottom branch
with everyone and an ant.

"What a day!" Piglet cried.

Elizabeth Ann only sighed.
So they sat down
with nary a frown
and told
stories of old.

And soon they went home
for tea and luncheon.

Made in the USA
Lexington, KY
17 April 2015